I0021626

Iot Arduino projects
Controlled Robot, Mugginess
and Temperature Measurement,
LPG Gas Leakage Detector,
Computerized Thermometer,
Programmed Door Opener etc,..

Copyright © Anbazhagan.k

All rights reserved 2019.

Iot Arduino projects like Gesture Controlled Robot, Mugginess and Temperature Measurement, LPG Gas Leakage Detector, Computerized Thermometer, Programmed Door Opener etc,..

CONTENTS

Acknowledgments

The writer might want to recognize the diligent work of the article group in assembling this book. He might likewise want to recognize the diligent work of the Raspberry Pi Foundation and the Arduino bunch for assembling items and networks that help to make the Internet of Things increasingly open to the overall population. Yahoo for the democratization of innovation!

Introduction

The Internet of Things (IOT) is a perplexing idea comprised of numerous PCs and numerous correspondence ways. Some IOT gadgets are associated with the Internet and some are most certainly not. Some IOT gadgets structure swarms that convey among themselves. Some are intended for a solitary reason, while some are increasingly universally useful PCs. This book is intended to demonstrate to you the IOT from the back to front. By structure IOT gadgets, the per user will comprehend the essential ideas and will almost certainly develop utilizing the rudiments to make his or her very own IOT applications. These included ventures will tell the per user the best way to assemble their very own IOT ventures and to develop the models appeared. The significance of Computer Security in IOT gadgets is additionally talked about and different systems for protecting the IOT from unapproved clients or programmers.

The most significant takeaway from this book is in structure the tasks yourself.

1. ACCELEROMETER BASED HAND GESTURE CONTROLLED ROBOT UTILIZING ARDUINO

Robots are assuming a significant job in mechanization over every one of the parts like development, military, medicinal, fabricating, and so on. In the wake of making some fundamental robots like line adherent robot, PC controlled robot, and so forth, we have built up this accelerometer based signal controlled robot by using arduino uno. In this undertaking we applied hand movement to drive the robot. For this reason we have utilized accelerometer which chips away at increasing speed.

Required Components

- Arduino UNO
- Accelerometer
- DC Motors
- HT12E

- HT12D
- Motor Driver L293D
- RF Pair
- Battery Connector
- 9 Volt Battery
- Robot Chasis
- USB cable

RF Pair:

A motion controlled robot is constrained by using hand rather than some other technique like gets or joystick. Here one simply needs to move hand to control the robot. A transmitting gadget is utilized in your grasp which contains RF Transmitter and accelerometer. This will transmit order to robot with the goal that it can do the necessary undertaking like pushing ahead, invert, turning left, turning right and stop. Every one of these errands will be performed by utilizing hand motion.

Here the most significant part is accelerometer. Accelerometer is a 3 pivot speeding up estimation gadget with +-3g territory. This gadget is made by using poly-silicon surface sensor as well as sign molding circuit to quantify quickening. The yield of this gadget is Analog in nature as well as corresponding to the speeding up. This device evaluates the static expanding rate of gravity when we tilt it. Likewise, gives a result in kind of development or vibration.

As indicated by the datasheet of adxl335 polysilicon surface-micromachined structure set over silicon wafer. Polysilicon springs suspend the structure through outside of the wafer as well as give an opposition against speeding up powers. Redirection of the structure is estimated utilizing a differential capacitor which consolidate autonomous fixed plates and plates connected to the moving mass. The rigid plates are driven by 180° out-of-stage square waves. Speeding up avoids the moving mass and unbalances the differential capacitor bringing about a sensor yield whose sufficiency is corresponding to increasing speed. Stage touchy demodulation systems are then used to decide the size and heading of the speeding up.

Stick Description of accelerometer

- Vcc 5 volt supply ought to associate at this stick.

- X-OUT This stick gives an Analog yield in x heading

- Y-OUT This stick give an Analog Output in y heading

- Z-OUT This stick gives an Analog Output in z bearing

- GND Ground

- ST This stick utilized for set affectability of sensor

Circuit Diagram and Explanation

Motion Controlled Robot is isolated into two areas:

- Transmitter part

- Recipient part

In transmitter section an accelerometer as well as a RF transmitter unit is utilized. As we have quite recently discussed that accelerometer gives a simple yield so here we have to change over this simple information in to computerized. For this reason we have utilized 4 direct comparator circuit instead of any ADC. By setting reference voltage we gets a computerized flag and afterward apply this sign to HT12E encoder to encode information or changing over it into sequential shape and afterward send this information by utilizing RF transmitter into the earth.

At the beneficiary end we have utilized RF recipient to get information and afterward applied to HT12D decoder. This decoder IC changes over got sequential information to parallel and afterward read by utilizing arduino. As indicated by got information we drive robot by utilizing two DC engine in forward, turn around, left, right and stop heading.

Working

Signal controlled robot moves as per hand development as we place transmitter in our grasp. At the point when we tilt turn in front side, robot start to pushing ahead and keeps pushing ahead until next order is given.

At the point when we tilt turn in reverse side, robot change its state and start moving in reverse heading until other direction is given.

At the point when we tilt it in left side Robot get turn left till next direction.

At the point when we tilt submit right side robot went to right.

Also, for halting robot we keeps turn in stable.

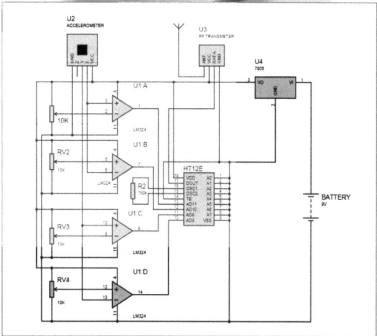

Circuit Diagram for Transmitter Section

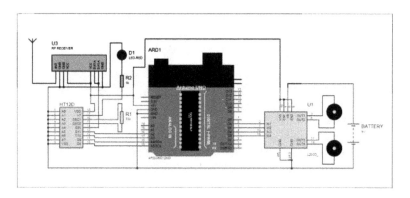

Circuit Diagram for Receiver Section

Circuit for this hand signal controlled robot is very basic. As appeared in above schematic outlines, a RF pair is utilized for correspondence and associated with arduino. Engine driver is associated with arduino to run the robot. Engine driver's info stick 2, 7, 10 and 15 is associated with arduino advanced stick number 6, 5, 4 and 3 separately. Here we have utilized two DC engines to drive robot in which one engine is associated at yield stick of engine driver 3 and 6 and another engine is associated at 11 and 14. A 9 volt Battery is likewise used to control the engine driver for driving engines.

Program Explanation

In program as a matter of first importance we have characterized yield pins for engines.

```
#define FD 16
#define BD 17
#define LD 18
#define RD 19

#define m11 3
#define m12 4
#define m21 5
#define m22 6
```

And afterward in arrangement we have given the headings to stick.

```
void setup()
{
  pinMode(FD, INPUT);
  pinMode(BD, INPUT);
  pinMode(LD, INPUT);
  pinMode(RD, INPUT);

  pinMode(m11, OUTPUT);
  pinMode(m12, OUTPUT);
  pinMode(m21, OUTPUT);
  pinMode(m22, OUTPUT);
```

After this we read contribution by utilizing 'if explanation' and perform relative activity.

```
int temp1=digitalRead(FD);
int temp2=digitalRead(BD);
int temp3=digitalRead(LD);
int temp4=digitalRead(RD);

if(temp1==1 && temp2==0 && temp3==0 && temp4==0)
backward();
```

There are all out five conditions for this Gesture controlled Robot which are giving beneath:

Movement of hand	Input for Arduino from gesture				
Side	D3	D2	D1	D0	Direction

Stable	0	0	0	0	Stop
Tilt right	0	0	0	1	Turn Right
Tilt left	0	0	1	0	Turn Left
Tilt back	1	0	0	0	Backward
Tilt front	0	1	0	0	Forward

We have writen the total program as indicated by the above table conditions. The following is the finished code.

Code

```
#define FD 16
#define BD 17
#define LD 18
#define RD 19
#define m11 3
#define m12 4
#define m21 5
#define m22 6
void forward()
{
  digitalWrite(m11, HIGH);
  digitalWrite(m12, LOW);
  digitalWrite(m21, HIGH);
  digitalWrite(m22, LOW);
}
void backward()
{
  digitalWrite(m11, LOW);
```

```
 digitalWrite(m12, HIGH);
 digitalWrite(m21, LOW);
 digitalWrite(m22, HIGH);
}
void left()
{
 digitalWrite(m11, HIGH);
 digitalWrite(m12, LOW);
 digitalWrite(m21, LOW);
 digitalWrite(m22, LOW);
}
void right()
{
 digitalWrite(m11, LOW);
 digitalWrite(m12, LOW);
 digitalWrite(m21, HIGH);
 digitalWrite(m22, LOW);
}
void Stop()
{
 digitalWrite(m11, LOW);
 digitalWrite(m12, LOW);
 digitalWrite(m21, LOW);
 digitalWrite(m22, LOW);
}
void setup()
{
 pinMode(FD, INPUT);
 pinMode(BD, INPUT);
 pinMode(LD, INPUT);
```

```
 pinMode(RD, INPUT);
 pinMode(m11, OUTPUT);
 pinMode(m12, OUTPUT);
 pinMode(m21, OUTPUT);
 pinMode(m22, OUTPUT);
}
void loop()
{
 int temp1 = digitalRead(FD);
 int temp2 = digitalRead(BD);
 int temp3 = digitalRead(LD);
 int temp4 = digitalRead(RD);


 if(temp1==1 && temp2==0 && temp3==0 &&
temp4==0)
 backward();
  else if(temp1==0 && temp2==1 && temp3==0 &&
temp4==0)
 forward();
  else if(temp1==0 && temp2==0 && temp3==1 &&
temp4==0)
 left();
  else if(temp1==0 && temp2==0 && temp3==0 &&
temp4==1)
 right();
 else
 Stop();
}
```

2. MUGGINESS AND TEMPERATURE MEASUREMENT UTILIZING ARDUINO

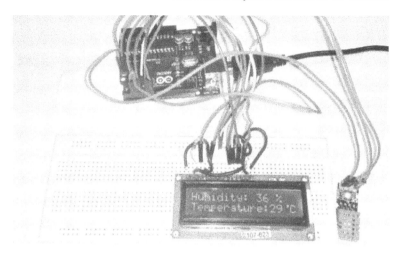

Mugginess and temperature are basic parameters to quantify natural conditions. In this Arduino based undertaking we are gonna to quantify surrounding temperature and mugginess and show it on a 16x2 LCD screen. A consolidated temperature and himidity sensor DHT11 is utilized with Arduino uno to build up this Celsius scale thermometer and rate scale mugginess estimation venture. In one of my past task, I have additionally built up an advanced thermometer utilizing temperature sensor LM35.

This undertaking comprises of three segments - one detects the dampness as well as temperature by utilizing mugginess and temperature sensor DHT11. The subsequent area peruses the DHTsensor module's yield and concentrates temperature and moistness esteems into an appropriate number in rate and Celsius scale. Also, the third piece of the framework shows stickiness and temperature on LCD.

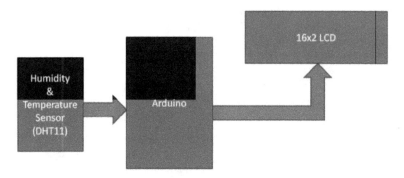

Working of this task depends on single wire sequential correspondence. Initially arduino send a beginning sign to DHT module as well as afterward DHT gives a reaction signal containing temperature as well as stickiness information. Arduino gather and concentrate in two sections one is dampness and second is temperature and afterward send them to 16x2 LCD.

Here in this task we have utilized a sensor module to be specific DHT11. This module includes a mugginess and temperature different with an adjusted advanced sign yield implies DHT11 sensor module is a consolidated module for detecting moistness and temperature which gives an aligned computerized yield signal. DHT11 gives us extremely exact estimation of moistness and temperature and guarantees high unwavering quality as well as long haul steadiness. This sensor has a resistive sort mugginess estimation segment and NTC type temperature estimation segment with a 8-piece microcontroller inbuilt which has a quick reaction and financially savvy and accessible in 4-stick single line bundle.

DHT 11 module deals with sequential correspondence for example single wire correspondence. This module sends information in type of heartbeat train of explicit timespan. Before sending information to arduino it needs some introduce order with a period delay. Also, the entire procedure time is about 4ms. A total information transmission is of 40-piece and information configuration of this procedure is given beneath:

8-piece indispensable RH information + 8-piece decimal RH information + 8-piece necessary T information + 8-piece decimal T information + 8-piece check total.

Complete Process

As a matter of first importance arduino sends a high to low begin sign to DHT 11 with 18 µs deferral to guarantee DHT's location. And afterward arduino pull-up the information line and sit tight for 20-40µs for DHT's reaction. Once DHT recognizes begins signal, it will send a low voltage level reaction sign to arduino of time delay about 80µs. And afterward DHT controller pull up the information line and keeps it for 80µs for DHT's organizing of sending information.

At the point when information transport is at low voltage level it implies that DHT11 is sending reaction signal. When it is done, DHT again makes information line pull-up for 80µs for getting ready information transmission.

Information group that is sending by DHT to arduino for each piece starts with 50µs low voltage level and length of high voltage level sign decides if information bit is "0" or "1".

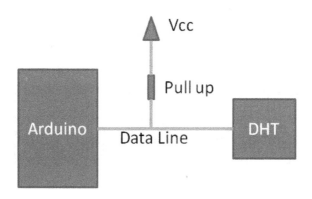

One significant thing is to ensure pull up resistor esteem provided that we are putting DHT sensor at <20 meter separation, 5k pull up resistor is suggested. In the event that setting DHT at longer the 20 meter, at that point utilize proper worth draw up resistor.

Circuit Diagram and Explanation

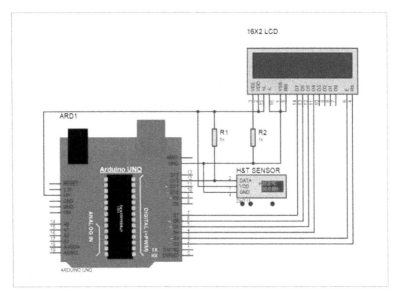

A fluid precious stone presentation is utilized for showing temperature and dampness which is straightforwardly associated with arduino in 4-piece mode. Pins of LCD to be specific RS, EN, D4, D5, D6 and D7 are associated with arduino advanced stick number 2, 3, 4, 5, 6 and 7. What's more, a DHT11 sensor module is additionally associated with computerized stick 12 of arduino with a 5k pull-up resistor.

Programming Description

In programming, we are gonna to utilize pre-constructed libraries for DHT11 sensor as well as LCD show

module.

```
#include<dht.h>
#include<LiquidCrystal.h>
```

At that point we haved characterized pins for LCD and DHT sensor as well as introduced every one of the things in arrangement. At that point in a circle by utilizing dht work peruses DHT sensor and afterward utilizing some dht capacities we remove stickiness and temperature and show them on LCD.

```
void loop()
{
  DHT.read11(dht_dpin);
  lcd.setCursor(0,0);
  lcd.print("Humidity: ");
  lcd.print(DHT.humidity);
  lcd.print(" %");
  lcd.setCursor(0,1);
  lcd.print("Temperature:");
  lcd.print(DHT.temperature);
```

Here degree image is made by utilizing custom character strategy.

```
byte degree[8] =
            {
                0b00011,
                0b00011,
                0b00000,
                0b00000,
                0b00000,
                0b00000,
                0b00000,
                0b00000
            };
```

Code

#include<dht.h>   // Including library for dht

```
#include<LiquidCrystal.h>
LiquidCrystal lcd(2, 3, 4, 5, 6, 7);
#define dht_dpin 12
dht DHT;
byte degree[8] =
     {
       0b00011,
       0b00011,
       0b00000,
       0b00000,
       0b00000,
       0b00000,
       0b00000,
       0b00000
     };
void setup()
{
lcd.begin(16, 2);
lcd.createChar(1, degree);
lcd.clear();
lcd.print(" Humidity ");
lcd.setCursor(0,1);
lcd.print(" Measurement ");
delay(2000);
lcd.clear();
lcd.print("Hello World ");
delay(2000);
}
void loop()
{
```

```
DHT.read11(dht_dpin);
lcd.setCursor(0,0);
lcd.print("Humidity: ");
 lcd.print(DHT.humidity);   // printing Humidity on
LCD
lcd.print(" %");
lcd.setCursor(0,1);
lcd.print("Temperature:");
lcd.print(DHT.temperature);  // Printing temperature
on LCD
lcd.write(1);
lcd.print("C");
delay(500);
}
```

◆ ◆ ◆

3.LED BLINKING WITH ARDUINO UNO

ARDUINO UNO is an ATMEGA controller based board intended for electronic designers and specialists. Arduino based program improvement condition is a simple method to compose the program when contrasted with other condition advancement programs.

Components Required

Equipment: Arduino uno board, associating pins, 220? resistor, LED, breadboard.

Programming: Arduino Nightly (https://www.arduino.cc/en/Main/Software)

Circuit Diagram and Working Explanation

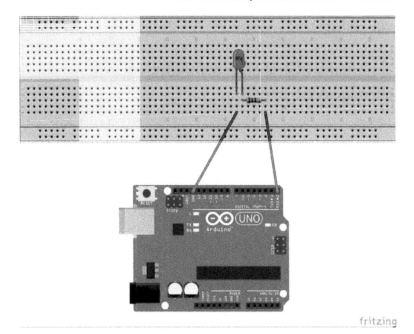

fritzing

Here we will compose a program to flicker a LED for each 500ms. In arduino uno, a LED will be now planned at the pin13, yet we won't utilize it. Here we will associate a demonstrating LED to PIN0 through a present restricting resistor.

The controller in arduino is as of now modified to chip away at outer gem. So we need not to stress over wire bits or anything. The arduino takes a shot at 16Mhz gem clock, which is as of now installed in the load up.

Code

// The setup function runs when you press reset or power the board

```
void setup()
{
//initialize digital pin 0 as an output.
pinMode(0, OUTPUT);
}
//the loop function runs over and over again forever
void loop()
{
digitalWrite(0, HIGH);  // turn the LED on (HIGH is the
voltage level)
delay(500);        // wait for a second
digitalWrite(0, LOW);   // turn the LED off by making
the voltage LOW
delay(500);        // wait for a second
}
```

4. PC CONTROLLED ROBOT UTILIZING ARDUINO

As a result of planning this line supporter robot utilizing arduino uno, I have built up this PC controlled robot. It very well may be controlled by means of the PC and we can utilize explicit console keys to move it. It runs over sequential correspondence which we have just examined in our past venture - PC Controlled Home Automation.

Components Required

- Arduino UNO
- DC Motor
- Laptop
- 9 Volt Battery
- Motor Driver L293D

- USB cable
- Battery Connector
- Robot Chasis

Concepts and Details

We can isolate this PC controlled robot circuit into various fragments and they are - sensor area, control segment and driver segment. Give us a chance to see them independently.

Direction or PC area: This segment has a sequential specialized gadget like PC, workstation and so on. Here in this undertaking we have utilized a PC for exhibit. We sends direction to arduino by composing a character on hyper terminal or some other sequential terminal like hyper terminal, Hercules, putty, arduino's sequential terminal and so forth.

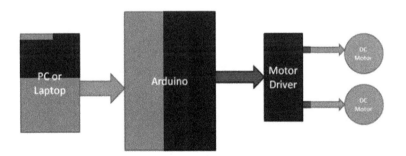

Control Section: Arduino UNO is utilized for controlling entire the procedure of robot. Arduino peruses directions sent by PC and contrast and characterized characters or directions. In case directions are coordinated, arduino sends suitable order to driver segment.

Driver segment: driver segment comprises a L293D engine driver IC and two DC engines. Engine driver is utilized for driving engines on the grounds that arduino doesn't supply enough voltage and flow to engine. So we add an engine driver circuit to get enough voltage and ebb and flow for engine. By gathering directions from arduino, engine driver drives engines as per directions.

Working

We have modified the PC controlled robot to run by certain directions that are send by means of sequential correspondence to arduino from PC. (see programming segment underneath)

At the point when we press 'f' or 'F', robot begin to push ahead and moving proceeds until next order is given.

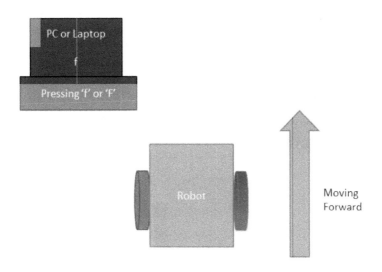

At the point when we press 'b' or 'B', robot change his state and start moving in reverse course until some other order is given.

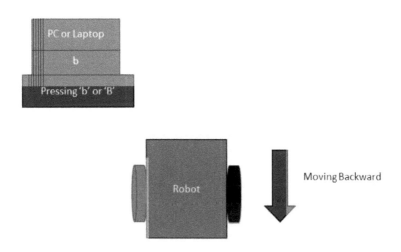

At the point when we press 'l' or 'L', Robot gets turn left

until the following direction.

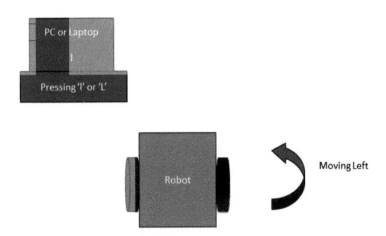

At the point when we press 'r" or 'R' robot goes to right.

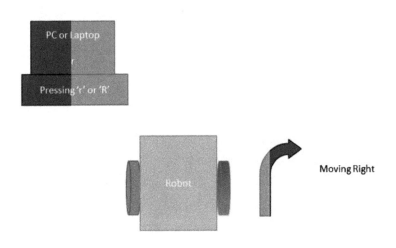

What's more, for halting robot we give 's' or 'S' order to arduino.

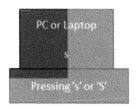

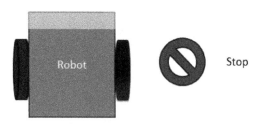

Circuit Diagram and Explanation

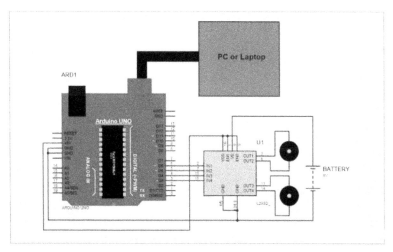

Circuit graph for Arduino based PC controlled robot is appeared in the above chart. Just an engine driver IC is associated with arduino for running robot. For sending order to robot we utilized inbuilt sequential information converter by utilizing USB link with workstation. Engine driver's info stick 2, 7, 10 and 15 is associated at arduino advanced stick number 6, 5, 4 and 3 individually. Here we have utilized two DC engines to driver robot in which one engine is associated at yield stick of engine driver 3 and 6 and another engine is associated at 11 and 14. A 9 volt Battery is utilized to control the engine driver for driving engines.

Program Explanation

In the programming most importantly we have characterized yield pins for engines.

```
#define m11 3
#define m12 4
#define m21 5
#define m22 6
```

And afterward in arrangement we have offered headings to stick and start sequential correspondence.

```
void setup()
{
  pinMode(m11, OUTPUT);
  pinMode(m12, OUTPUT);
  pinMode(m21, OUTPUT);
  pinMode(m22, OUTPUT);
  Serial.begin(9600);
}
```

After that we read sequential cushion by perusing "serial.read()" work and get its incentive in to a transitory variable. And afterward coordinate it with characterized directions by utilizing "if" proclamation to work the robot.

```
void loop()
{
  while(Serial.available())
  {
    char In=Serial.read();

    if(In=='f' || In=='F')              // Forward
    {
      digitalWrite(ml1, HIGH);
      digitalWrite(ml2, LOW);
      digitalWrite(m21, HIGH);
      digitalWrite(m22, LOW);
```

There are four conditions to move this PC controlled Robot that are given in beneath table.

Input Commands		Output				Movement of Robot
		Left Motor		Right Motor		
		1.	1.	1.	1.	
S.	1.	1.	1.	1.	1.	Stop
1.	1.	1.	1.	1.	1.	Turn Right
1.	1.	1.	1.	1.	1.	Turn Left
1.	1.	1.	1.	1.	1.	Backward
1.	1.	1.	1.	1.	1.	Forward

We have composed the program as indicated by above table conditions. Complete code is given beneath.

Code

```
#define m11 3
#define m12 4
#define m21 5
#define m22 6
void setup()
{
 pinMode(m11, OUTPUT);
 pinMode(m12, OUTPUT);
 pinMode(m21, OUTPUT);
 pinMode(m22, OUTPUT);
 Serial.begin(9600);
}
void loop()
{
 while(Serial.available())
 {
  char In=Serial.read();

   if(In=='f' || In=='F')      // Forward
  {
   digitalWrite(m11, HIGH);
   digitalWrite(m12, LOW);
   digitalWrite(m21, HIGH);
   digitalWrite(m22, LOW);
  }

   else if(In=='b' || In=='B')       //backward
  {
   digitalWrite(m11, LOW);
```

```
 digitalWrite(m12, HIGH);
 digitalWrite(m21, LOW);
 digitalWrite(m22, HIGH);
}


   else if(In=='l' || In=='L')   // Left
{
 digitalWrite(m11, HIGH);
 digitalWrite(m12, LOW);
 digitalWrite(m21, LOW);
 digitalWrite(m22, LOW);
}


   else if(In=='r' || In=='R')   // Right
{
 digitalWrite(m11, LOW);
 digitalWrite(m12, LOW);
 digitalWrite(m21, HIGH);
 digitalWrite(m22, LOW);
}


   else if(In=='s' || In=='S')   // stop
{
 digitalWrite(m11, LOW);
 digitalWrite(m12, LOW);
 digitalWrite(m21, LOW);
 digitalWrite(m22, LOW);
}
```

```
    else
  {

    }
 }
}
```

◆ ◆ ◆

5. PROGRAMMED DOOR OPENER UTILIZING ARDUINO

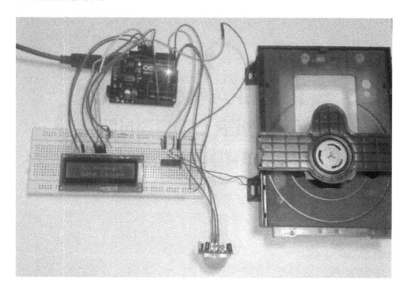

You probably observed programmed entryway openers in shopping centers and other business structures. They open the entryway when somebody draws close to the passage and close it after at some point. Various advancements are accessible to make such sorts of frameworks like PIR sensors, Radar sensors, Laser sensors, Infrared sensors, and so forth. In this arduino based undertaking, we have attempted to imitate a similar framework by utilizing a PIR sensor.

It utilizes a movement identifying sensor (PIR sensor) to open or close the entryway which identifies the infrared vitality overlooked from human's body. At the point when somebody comes before the entryway, the infrared vitality distinguished by the sensor changes and it triggers the sensor to open the entryway at whatever point somebody moves toward the entryway. The sign is additionally sent to arduino uno that controls the entryway.

Circuit Components

- Arduino UNO
- CD case (DVD Troly)
- 16x2 LCD
- Connecting wires
- PIR Sensor
- 1 k resistor
- Bread board
- Motor driver
- Power supply

PIR Sensor

PIR sensor identifies any adjustment in heat, and at whatever point it recognizes any change, its yield PIN turns out to be HIGH. They are likewise alluded as Pyroelectric or IR movement sensors.

Here we should take note of that each article discharges some measure of infrared when warmed. Human additionally emanates infrared in light of body heat. PIR sensors can recognize modest quantity of variety in infrared. At whatever point an item goes through the sensor go, it produces infrared as a result of the contact among air and question, and get captured by PIR.

The fundamental segment of PIR sensor is Pyroelectric sensor appeared in figure (rectangular precious stone behind the plastic top). Alongside BISS0001 ("Micro Power PIR Motion Detector IC"), a few resistors, capacitors and different segments used to fabricate PIR sensor. BISS0001 IC take the contribution from sensor and does handling to make the yield stick HIGH or LOW in like manner.

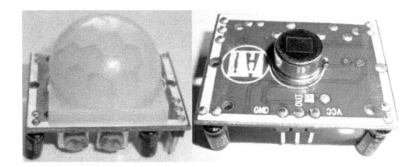

Pyroelectric sensor isolate in two parts, when there is no movement, the two parts stay in same state, implies the two detects a similar degree of infrared. When someone enters in first a large portion of, the infrared degree of one half gets more prominent than other, and this causes PIRs to respond and makes the yield stick high.

Pyroelectric sensor is secured by a plastic top, which has cluster of numerous Fresnel Lens inside. These focal points are bended in such a way in this way, that sensor can cover a wide range.

Circuit Diagram and Explanation

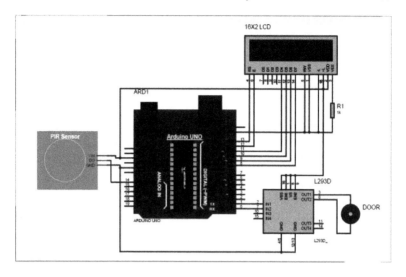

Associations for arduino based entryway opener circuit are showed in the above chart. Here a PIR sensor is utilized for detecting human movement which has three terminals Vcc, GND as well as Dout. Dout is straightforwardly associated with stick number 14 (A0) of arduino uno. A 16x2 LCD is utilized for showing the status. RS, EN pins of LCD associated with 13 and 12 of arduino and information pins D0-D7 are associated with arduino computerized stick numbers 11, 10, 9, 8. RW is legitimately associated with ground. L293D engine driver is associated with arduino stick 0 and 1 for opening and shutting the entryway. Here in circuit we have utilized an engine for door.

Programming Explanation

The idea utilized here for writing computer programs is extremely basic. In program we have just utilized advanced information yield.

DigitalRead is utilized for perusing yield of PIR sensor.

```
if(digitalRead(PIR_sensor))
{
  lcd.setCursor(0,0);
  lcd.print("Movement Detected");
  lcd.setCursor(0, 1);
  lcd.print("    Gate Opened    ");
  digitalWrite(m11, HIGH);
  digitalWrite(m12, LOW);
```

Since forward, in the case PIR sensor detects any movement, at that point program sends an order to open entryway, stop door, shutting door and stop door.

```
lcd.print("    Gate Opened    ");
digitalWrite(m11, HIGH);            // gate opening
digitalWrite(m12, LOW);
delay(1000);
digitalWrite(m11, LOW);             // gate stop for a while
digitalWrite(m12, LOW);
delay(1000);
lcd.clear();
lcd.print("    Gate Closed    ");
digitalWrite(m11, LOW);             // gate closing
digitalWrite(m12, HIGH);
delay(1000);
digitalWrite(m11, LOW);             // gate closed
digitalWrite(m12, LOW);
delay(1000);
```

See underneath the total code for arduino based programmed entryway opener.

Code

#include <LiquidCrystal.h>
LiquidCrystal lcd(13, 12, 11, 10, 9, 8);
#define PIR_sensor 14
#define m11 0
#define m12 1
void setup()

```
{
 lcd.begin(16, 2);
 pinMode(m11, OUTPUT);
 pinMode(m12, OUTPUT);
 pinMode(PIR_sensor, INPUT);
 lcd.print(" Automatic ");
 lcd.setCursor(0,1);
 lcd.print(" Door Opener ");
 delay(3000);
 lcd.clear();
 lcd.print("Hello_world ");
 delay(2000);
}
void loop()
{
 if(digitalRead(PIR_sensor))
 {
  lcd.setCursor(0,0);
  lcd.print("Movement Detected");
  lcd.setCursor(0, 1);
  lcd.print(" Gate Opened ");
  digitalWrite(m11, HIGH);    // gate opening
  digitalWrite(m12, LOW);
  delay(1000);
  digitalWrite(m11, LOW);     // gate stop for a while
  digitalWrite(m12, LOW);
  delay(1000);
  lcd.clear();
  lcd.print(" Gate Closed ");
  digitalWrite(m11, LOW);      // gate closing
```

```
digitalWrite(m12, HIGH);
delay(1000);
digitalWrite(m11, LOW);        // gate closed
digitalWrite(m12, LOW);
delay(1000);
}


else
{
lcd.setCursor(0,0);
lcd.print(" No Movement ");
lcd.setCursor(0,1);
lcd.print(" Gate Closed ");
digitalWrite(m11, LOW);
digitalWrite(m12, LOW);
}
}
```

◆ ◆ ◆

6. ADVANCED DICE UTILIZING ARDUINO

We as a whole know about shakers and frequently played LUDO or SANP SIDI (Snake and Ladders) game by utilizing dice. Shakers is a squire type strong box which contains 6 unique numbers on the entirety of its sides. We toss dice on a surface to get an arbitrary number while playing the games. In this undertaking we have tried to duplicate it with a computerized shakers utilizing arduino uno board. Instead of tossing the bones, here we have to press a catch to get an arbitrary number between 0 to 6.

Required Components

- Arduino UNO
- Seven segment display (Common Anode)
- Push buttons
- Connecting wires
- Bread board

- 1 k resistor
- Power supply

Circuit Diagram and Explanation

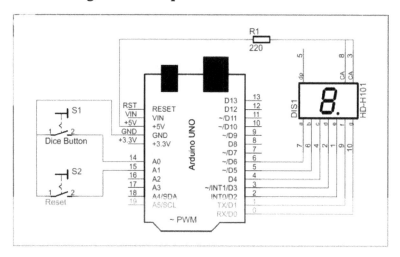

As appeared in the above computerized dice circuit, arduino is utilized for controlling entire the procedure. Two push catches are utilized in the circuit - one to begin the bones and other for resetting the shakers. Arduino peruses these two fastens and play out the activity. A seven portion show is utilized to show the bones result.

Arduino is ceaselessly executing rand() work and put away its incentive in to a transitory variable. At the point when shakers button is get squeezed put away worth determined and show on seven portion by utilizing suitable technique (see programming some portion of article).

Here in this shakers circuit, a typical anode seven section show is utilized for showing dice numbers, which is legitimately associated with arduino advanced stick numbers 6, 5, 4, 3, 2, 1, 0. Also, regular anode stick of seven section is associated with +5 volt 220 Ohm resistor. Two push button are additionally associated to be specific dice fasten and reset button which are associated with advanced stick 14 (A0) and 15 (A1) as for ground.

Code Explanation

Programming some portion of this venture assumes a significant job to show irregular advanced shakers number on seven section show. Arduino doesn't contain any library for seven portion show. so we made entire code without utilizing any library.

Most importantly we chooses computerized stick for seven section show.

```
int pin[7]={6,5,4,3,2,1,0};
```

After it we make a variety of 6 digits of bones in particular 1, 2, 3, 4, 5 and 6.

```
char digit[6]={0x02,0x79,0x24,0x30,0x19,0x12};
```

Presently we provided guidance to utilize arduino

stick as yield.

```
void setup()

{

 for(int i=0;i<7;i++)

 pinMode(pin[i], OUTPUT);

 pinMode(dice, INPUT);

 pinMode(resett, INPUT);

 digitalWrite(dice, HIGH);

 digitalWrite(resett, HIGH);
```

We send a code for showing zero on seven section show as a matter of course.

```
int temp=0x40;

   for(int i=0;i<7;i++)

   {

     int temp1=temp&0x01;
```

```
    digitalWrite(pin[i], temp1);

    temp=temp>>1;

}
```

Presently we run rand() capacity to get an arbitrary number.

```
int temp=rand();
```

What's more, when we press the shakers button program first guide this arbitrary number and afterward send number to seven fragment show by utilizing bit savvy administrator.

```
if(digitalRead(dice)==0)

{

    int k=temp%6;

    temp=digit[k];

    wait();

    for(int i=0;i<7;i++)

    {
```

```
    int temp1=temp&0x01;

    digitalWrite(pin[i], temp1);

    temp=temp>>1;

  }

  delay(200);

}
```

Furthermore, same for reset button.

In this program we sends single piece at once. Here we applying a for circle which run 7 time to send information to each portion individually.

Code

```
#define resett 15
#define dice 14
char digit[6]={0x02, 0x79, 0x24, 0x30, 0x19, 0x12};
int pin[7]={6,5,4,3,2,1,0};
void setup()
{
 for(int i=0;i<7;i++)
 pinMode(pin[i], OUTPUT);
 pinMode(dice, INPUT);
 pinMode(resett, INPUT);
 digitalWrite(dice, HIGH);
```

```
  digitalWrite(resett, HIGH);
  int temp=0x40;
  for(int i=0;i<7;i++)
  {
   int temp1=temp&0x01;
   digitalWrite(pin[i], temp1);
   temp=temp>>1;
  }
  delay(1000);
}
void loop()
{
 int temp=rand();
 if(digitalRead(dice)==0)
 {
  int k=temp%6;
  temp=digit[k];
  wait();
  for(int i=0;i<7;i++)
  {
   int temp1=temp&0x01;
   digitalWrite(pin[i], temp1);
   temp=temp>>1;
  }
  delay(200);
 }


  if(digitalRead(resett)==0)
 {
  temp=0x40;
```

```
 for(int i=0;i<7;i++)
 {
  int temp1=temp&0x01;
  digitalWrite(pin[i], temp1);
  temp=temp>>1;
 }
}
}
void wait()
{
 for(int m=0;m<10;m++)
 {
 for(int k=0;k<6;k++)
 {
  int ch=digit[k];
  for(int l=0;l<7;l++)
  {
   char tem2=ch&0x01;
   digitalWrite(pin[l], tem2);
   ch=ch>>1;
  }
  delay(50);
 }
 }
}
```

7. ARDUINO AND ULTRASONIC SENSOR BASED DISTANCE MEASUREMENT

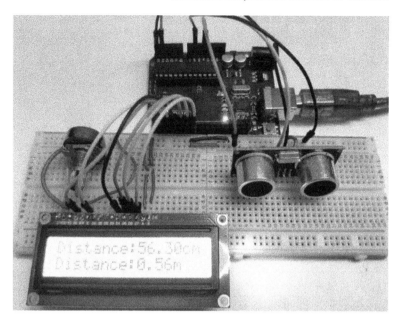

Ultrasonic sensors are extraordinary devices to quantify separation without genuine contact and utilized at a few places like water level estimation, separation estimation and so forth. This is an effective method to quantify little separations accurately. Here we have utilized a Ultrasonic Sensor to decide the division of a deterrent from the sensor. Essential head of ultrasonic separation estimation depends on ECHO. At the point when sound waves are transmitted in condition at that point waves are return back to source as ECHO subsequent to striking on the snag. So we just require to ascertain the voyaging time of the two sounds implies active time and returning time to cause subsequent to striking on the impediment. As speed of the sound is known to us, after some figuring we can ascertain the separation.

Components Used

- Arduino Uno or Pro Mini
- 16x2 LCD
- Ultrasonic sensor Module
- Bread board
- Scale
- Connecting wires
- 9 volt battery

Ultrasonic Sensor Module

Ultrasonic sensor HC-SR04 is used here to quantify separation in scope of 2cm-400cm with exactness of 3mm. The sensor module includes of ultrasonic transmitter, collector and the control circuit. The working standard of ultrasonic sensor is as per the following:

- Significant level signal is sent for 10us utilizing Trigger.

- The module sends eight 40 KHz flag naturally, and afterward recognizes whether heartbeat is gotten or not.

- On the off chance that the sign is gotten, at that point it is through elevated level. The hour of high length is the time hole among sending and getting the sign.

Distance= (Time x Speed of Sound in Air (340 m/s))/2

Timing Diagram

The module takes a shot at the regular wonder of ECHO of sound. A heartbeat is sent for about 10us to trigger the module. After which the module consequently sends 8 cycles of 40 KHz ultrasound sign and checks its reverberation. The sign in the wake of hitting with a hindrance returns back and is caught by the beneficiary. Along these lines the separation of the obstruction from the sensor is basically determined by the recipe given as

Distance = (time x speed)/2.

Here we have partitioned the result of speed and time by 2 on the grounds that the time is the complete time it took to arrive at the impediment and return back.

Along these lines an opportunity to arrive at snag is simply a wide area of the complete time taken.

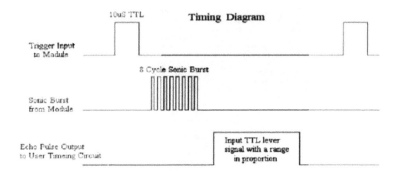

Ultrasonic Sensor Arduino Circuit Diagram and Explanation

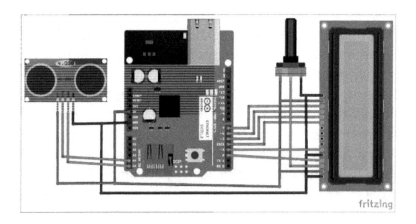

The circuit outline for arduino and ultrasonic sensor is appeared above to gauge the separation. In circuit associations Ultrasonic sensor module's "trigger" and "reverberation" pins are straightforwardly associated with stick 18(A4) and 19(A5) of arduino. A 16x2 LCD is associated with arduino in 4-piece mode. Control stick RS, RW and En are straightforwardly associated with arduino stick 2, GND and 3. Also, information stick D4-D7 is associated with 4, 5, 6 as well as 7 of arduino.

As a matter of first importance we have to trigger the ultrasonic sensor module to transmit signal by utilizing arduino and afterward hang tight for get ECHO. Arduino peruses the time among activating and Received ECHO. We realize that speed of sound is around 340m per s. so we can figure separation by utilizing given equation:

Distance= (travel time/2) * speed of sound

Where speed of sound around 340m every second.

A 16x2 LCD is utilized for showing separation.

Discover increasingly about the working of separation estimation venture in this instructional exercise: Distance estimation utilizing ultrasonic sensor.

https://hellothisisanbazhagan.com/sites/default/ files/projectimage_mic/Arduino-Distance-Sensor.jpg

Arduino Ultrasonic Sensor Code for Distance Measurement

In code we read time by utilizing pulseIn(pin). And afterward perform counts and showed result on 16x2 LCD by utilizing proper capacities.

```
digitalWrite(trigger,HIGH);
delayMicroseconds(10);
digitalWrite(trigger,LOW);
delayMicroseconds(2);
time=pulseIn(echo,HIGH);
distance=time*340/20000;
lcd.clear();
lcd.print("Distance:");
lcd.print(distance);
lcd.print("cm");
```

Code

```
#include <LiquidCrystal.h>


#define trigger 18
#define echo 19


LiquidCrystal lcd(2,3,4,5,6,7);


float time=0,distance=0;


void setup()
{
lcd.begin(16,2);
pinMode(trigger,OUTPUT);
pinMode(echo,INPUT);
lcd.print(" Ultra sonic");
lcd.setCursor(0,1);
lcd.print("Distance Meter");
delay(2000);
lcd.clear();
lcd.print(" Hello World");
```

```
delay(2000);
}


void loop()
{
lcd.clear();
digitalWrite(trigger,LOW);
delayMicroseconds(2);
digitalWrite(trigger,HIGH);
delayMicroseconds(10);
digitalWrite(trigger,LOW);
delayMicroseconds(2);
time=pulseIn(echo,HIGH);
distance=time*340/20000;
lcd.clear();
lcd.print("Distance:");
lcd.print(distance);
lcd.print("cm");
lcd.setCursor(0,1);
lcd.print("Distance:");
lcd.print(distance/100);
lcd.print("m");
delay(1000);
}
```

◆ ◆ ◆

8. LPG GAS LEAKAGE DETECTOR UTILIZING ARDUINO

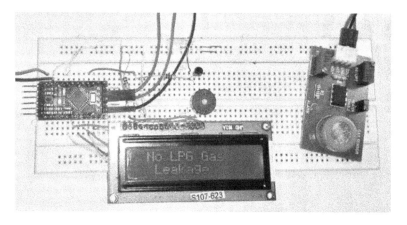

While LPG is a basic need of each family, its spillage could prompt a fiasco. To alarm on LPG spillage and forestall any mishappening there are different items to distinguish the spillage. Here we have built up an Arduino based LPG gas identifier caution. In case gas spillage happens, this framework recognizes it and makes a caution by buzing the bell appended with the circuit. This framework is anything but difficult to construct and any individual who have some information on hardware and programing, can manufacture it..

We have utilized a Lliquefied Petroleum Gas sensor module to identify LPG Gas. When LPG gas spillage happens, it gives a HIGH heartbeat on its DO stick and arduino ceaselessly peruses its DO stick. When Arduino gets a HIGH heartbeat from LPG Gas module it shows "LPG Gas Leakage Alert" message on 16x2 LCD and actuates bell which signals over and over until the gas indicator module doesn't detect the gas in condition. When LPG gas identifier module gives LOW heartbeat to arduino, at that point LCD shows "No LPG Gas Leakage" message.

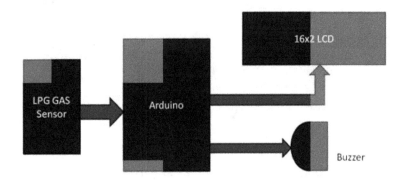

Components Used

- Arduino Pro Mini
- Buzzer
- Liquified Petroleum Gas sensor Module
- 16x2 LCD
- BC 547 Transistor
- Bread board
- 1K resistor
- Connecting wires
- 9 volt battery

LPG Gas Sensor Module

This module contains a MQ3 sensor which really recognizes LPG gas, a comparator (LM393) for contrasting MQ3 yield voltage and reference voltage. It provides a HIGH yield when LPG gas is detected. A potentiometer is likewise utilized for controlling affectability of gas detecting. This module is extremely simple to interface with microcontrollers and arduino and effectively accessible in showcase by name "LPG Gas Sensor Module". We can likewise manufacture it by utilizing LM358 or LM393 as well as MQ3.

Circuit Diagram and Description

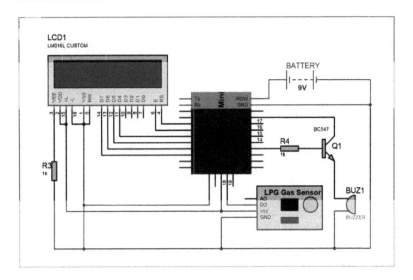

As appeared in the schematic graph above, it contains Arduino board, LPG GAS Sensor Module, bell and 16x2 LCD module. Arduino controls the entire procedure of this framework like perusing LPG Gas sensor module yield, sending message to LCD and actuating ringer. We can set affectability of this sensor module by inbuilt potentiometer put on it.

LPG gas sensor module's DO stick is straightforwardly associated with stick 18 (A4) of Arduino and Vcc and GND are associated with Vcc and GND of arduino. LPG gas sensor module comprise a MQ3 sensor which identifies LPG gas. This MQ3 sensor has a warmer inside which needs some radiator supply to warm up and it might takes as long as 15 moment to prepare for distinguishing LPG gas. What's more, a comparator circuit is utilized for changing over Analog yield of MQ3 in computerized. A 16x2 LCD is associated with arduino in 4-

piece mode. Control stick RS, RW and En are straightforwardly associated with arduino stick 2, GND and 3. What's more, information stick D0-D7 are associated with 4, 5, 6, 7 of arduino. A signal is associated with arduino stick number 13 through a NPN BC547 transistor having a 1 k resistor at its base.

Program Description

In programming we have utilized advanced perused capacity to peruse yield of LPG gas sensor module and afterward performed activity as indicated by input.

```
if(digitalRead(lpg_sensor))
{
  digitalWrite(buzzer, HIGH);
  lcd.clear();
  lcd.print("LPG Gas Leakage");
```

For testing this task we have utilized a cigarette lighter which contains LPG gas.

Code

```
#include <LiquidCrystal.h>
LiquidCrystal lcd(3, 2, 4, 5, 6, 7);
#define lpg_sensor 18
#define buzzer 13
void setup()
{
 pinMode(lpg_sensor, INPUT);
 pinMode(buzzer, OUTPUT);
 lcd.begin(16, 2);
```

```
lcd.print("LPG Gas Detector");
lcd.setCursor(0,1);
lcd.print("Hello World");
delay(2000);
}
void loop()
{
 if(digitalRead(lpg_sensor))
 {
  digitalWrite(buzzer, HIGH);
  lcd.clear();
  lcd.print("LPG Gas Leakage");
  lcd.setCursor(0, 1);
  lcd.print("  Alert  ");
  delay(400);
  digitalWrite(buzzer, LOW);
  delay(500);
 }

  else
 {
  digitalWrite(buzzer, LOW);
  lcd.clear();
  lcd.print(" No LPG Gas ");
  lcd.setCursor(0,1);
  lcd.print(" Leakage ");
  delay(1000);
 }
}
```

9. LINE FOLLOWER ROBOT UTILIZING ARDUINO

Line supporter Robot is a machine which pursues a line, either a dark line or white line. Fundamentally there are two types of line devotee robots: one is dark line adherent which pursues dark line and second is white line supporter which pursues white line. Line supporter really faculties the line and run over it.

Concepts of Line Follower

Idea of working of line supporter is identified with light. We use here the conduct of light at highly contrasting surface. At the point when light fall on a white surface it is practically full reflected and in the event of dark surface light is totally assimilated. This conduct of light is utilized in building a line devotee robot.

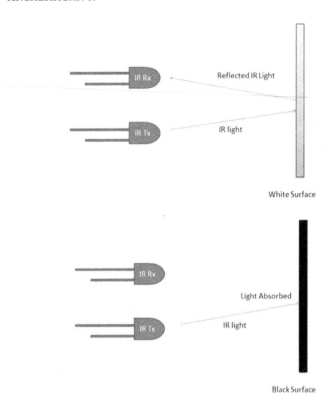

In this arduino based line devotee robot we have utilized IR Transmitters and IR recipients additionally called photograph diodes. They are utilized for sending and getting light. Infrared transmits infrared lights. At the point when infrared beams falls on white surface, it's reflected back and catched by photodiodes which produces some voltage changes. At the point when Infrared light falls on a dark surface, light is ingest by the dark surface and no beams are reflected back, subsequently photograph diode doesn't get any light or beams.

Here in this arduino line devotee robot when sensor detects white surface then arduino gets 1 as information and when detects dark line arduino gets 0 as information.

Circuit Explanation

The entire arduino line devotee robot can be partitioned into 3 areas: sensor segment, control segment and driver segment.

Sensor area:

This area contains Infrared diodes, potentiometer, Comparator (Op-Amp) as well as LED's. Potentiometer is utilized for setting reference voltage at comparator's one terminal and IR sensors are utilized to detect the line and give an adjustment in voltage at comparator's subsequent terminal. At that point comparator looks at the two voltages and produces a computerized sign at yield. Here in this line devotee circuit we have utilized two comparator for 2 sensors. LM358 is utilized as comparator. LM358 has inbuilt 2 low clamor Op-amps.

Control Section:

Arduino Pro Mini is utilized for controlling entire the procedure of line supporter robot. The yields of comparators are associated with computerized stick number 2 and 3 of arduino. Arduino read these sign and send directions to driver circuit to drive line devotee.

Driver area:

Driver area comprises engine driver and two DC engines. Engine driver is utilized for driving engines in light of the fact that arduino doesn't supply enough voltage and ebb and flow to engine. So we add an engine driver circuit to get enough voltage and ebb and flow for engine. Arduino sends directions to this engine driver and afterward it drive engines.

Working of Line Follower Robot using Arduino

Working of line adherent is exceptionally fascinating. Line adherent robot detects dark line by utilizing sensor and afterward sends the sign to arduino. At that point arduino drives the engine as per sensors' yield.

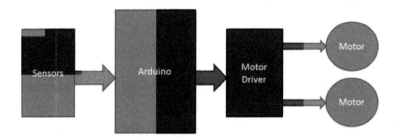

Here in this task we are utilizing two IR sensor modules to be specific left sensor and right sensor. At the point when both left and right sensor detects white then robot push ahead.

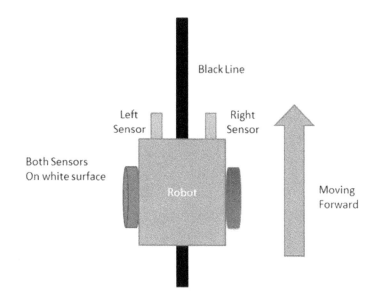

Whenever left sensor goes ahead dark line then robot turn left side.

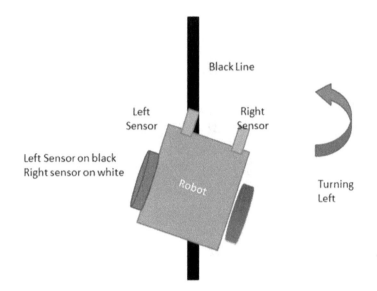

In case correct sensor sense dark line, at that point robot turn right side until both sensor comes at white surface. At the point when white surface comes robot begins proceeding onward forward once more.

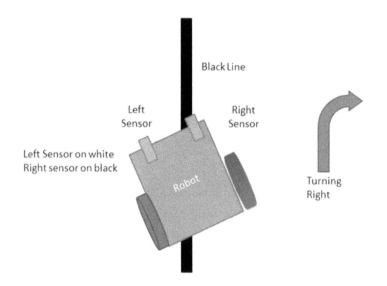

In the event that the two sensors goes ahead dark line, robot stops.

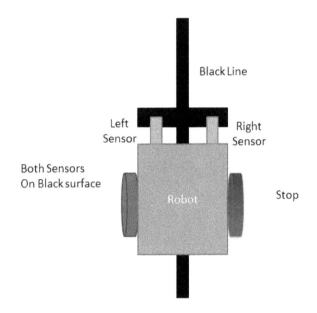

Black Line

Left
Sensor

Right
Sensor

Both Sensors
On Black surface

Robot

Stop

Circuit Diagram

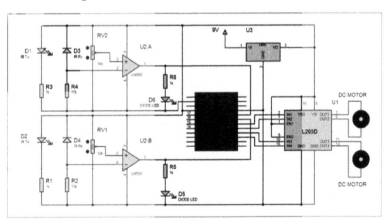

Complete circuit chart for arduino line supporter robot is appeared in the above iamge. As should be obvious yield of comparators is straightforwardly associated with arduino advanced stick number 2 and 3. Furthermore, engine driver's information stick 2, 7, 10 and 15 is associated with arduino's computerized stick number 4, 5, 6 and 7 individually. What's more, one engine is associated at yield stick of engine driver 3 and 6 and another engine is associated at stick 11 and 14.

Program Explanation

In program, above all else we characterized information and yield stick, and afterward in circle we checks inputs and sends yield as indicated by contributions to yield stick for driving engine. For checking input stick we utilized "if" proclamations.

```
/*-------definning Inputs------*/
#define LS 2        // left sensor
#define RS 3        // right sensor

/*-------definning Outputs------*/
#define LM1 4       // left motor
#define LM2 5       // left motor
#define RM1 6       // right motor
#define RM2 7       // right motor
```

There are four conditions in this line following robot that we read by utilizing arduino. We have utilized two sensor to be specific left sensor and right sensor.

Input		Output				Movement
Left Sensor	Right Sensor	Left Motor		Right Motor		Of Robot
LS	RS	LM1	LM2	RM1	RM2	
0	0	0	0	0	0	Stop
0	1	1	0	0	0	Turn Right

1	0	0	0	1	0	Turn Left
1	1	1	0	1	0	Forward

We compose the arduino line supporter code as per the conditions appeared in table above.

Required Components

Arduino

In our Project we have utilized a microcontroller to control entire the procedure of framework that is AR-DUINO. Arduino is an unhindered access equipment and extremely helpful for venture advancements. There are numerous sorts of arduino like Arduino UNO, arduino mega, arduino master smaller than normal, Lilypad and so on accessible in the market. Here we have utilized arduino ace smaller than usual in this venture as arduino star scaled down is little thus bread-board good. To consume program we have utilized FTDI burner.

L293D Motor Driver

L293D is an engine driver IC which has two channels for driving two engines. L293D has two inbuilt Transistor Darlington pair for current intensification and a different power supply stick for giving outer inventory to engines.

IR Module:

IR Module is sensor circuit which comprises IR LED/ photodiode pair, potentiometer, LM358, resistors and LED. IR sensor transmits Infrared light and photograph diode gets the infrared light.

Power Supply

I have added a voltage controller to get 5 volt for arduino, comparator and engine driver. Furthermore, a 9 volt battery is utilized to control the circuit.

Code

```
/*------ Arduino Line Follower Code----- */
/*-------definning Inputs------*/
#define LS 2    // left sensor
#define RS 3    // right sensor
/*-------definning Outputs------*/
#define LM1 4    // left motor
#define LM2 5    // left motor
#define RM1 6    // right motor
#define RM2 7    // right motor
void setup()
{
 pinMode(LS, INPUT);
 pinMode(RS, INPUT);
```

```
 pinMode(LM1, OUTPUT);
 pinMode(LM2, OUTPUT);
 pinMode(RM1, OUTPUT);
 pinMode(RM2, OUTPUT);
}
void loop()
{
 if(digitalRead(LS) && digitalRead(RS))    // Move For-
ward
 {
  digitalWrite(LM1, HIGH);
  digitalWrite(LM2, LOW);
  digitalWrite(RM1, HIGH);
  digitalWrite(RM2, LOW);
 }


 if(!(digitalRead(LS)) && digitalRead(RS))     // Turn
right
 {
  digitalWrite(LM1, LOW);
  digitalWrite(LM2, LOW);
  digitalWrite(RM1, HIGH);
  digitalWrite(RM2, LOW);
 }


 if(digitalRcad(LS) && !(digitalRead(RS)))   //turn left
 {
  digitalWrite(LM1, HIGH);
  digitalWrite(LM2, LOW);
```

```
  digitalWrite(RM1, LOW);
  digitalWrite(RM2, LOW);
}


  if(!(digitalRead(LS)) && !(digitalRead(RS)))   // stop
  {
  digitalWrite(LM1, LOW);
  digitalWrite(LM2, LOW);
  digitalWrite(RM1, LOW);
  digitalWrite(RM2, LOW);
  }
}
```

◆ ◆ ◆

10. COMPUTERIZED THERMOMETER UTILIZING ARDUINO AND LM35 TEMPERATURE SENSOR

Thermometers are valuable device being utilized from long time for temperature estimation. In this task we have made an Arduino based computerized thermometer to show the current surrounding temperature as well as temperature changes on a LCD unit progressively . It very well may be sent in houses, workplaces, enterprises and so on to gauge the temperature. This undertaking depends on Arduino which imparts here with LM35 temperature sensor and a 16x2 presentation unit. We can separate this arduino based thermometer into three segments - The principal detects the temperature by utilizing temperature sensor LM 35, second area changes over the temperature esteem into an appropriate numbers in Celsius scale which is finished by Arduino, and last piece of framework shows temperature on LCD. The equivalent is exhibited in beneath square outline.

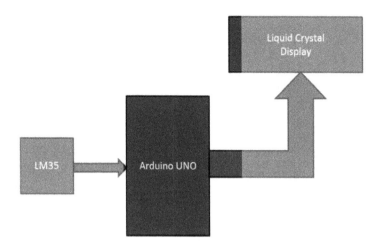

In this Arduino LM35 temperature sensor interfacing, Arduino Uno is utilized to control the entire procedure. A LM35 temperature sensor is utilized for detecting condition temperature which gives 1 degree temperature on each 10mV change at its yield stick. You can undoubtedly check it with voltmeter by interfacing Vcc at stick 1 and Ground at stick 3 and yield voltage at stick 2 of LM35 sensor. For a model if the yield voltage of LM35 sensor is 250m volt, that implies the temperature is around 25 degree Celsius.

Arduino peruses yield voltage of temperature sensor by utilizing Analog stick A0 and plays out the computation to change over this Analog incentive to a com puterized estimation of current temperature. After estimations arduino sends these figurings or temperature to 16x2 LCD unit by utilizing suitable directions of LCD.

Circuit Components

Arduino

In this task we have utilized a microcontroller to control entire the procedure of framework that is AR-DUINO board. As a matter of fact arduino is certainly not a unimportant controller as it has a working framework or boot-loader which runs on AVR controllers. Arduino is an unhindered access equipment stage and helpful for venture advancement reason. There are numerous sorts of arduino sheets like Arduino UNO, arduino mega, arduino expert small scale, Lilypad and so on are accessible in the market or you can likewise fabricate one without anyone else.

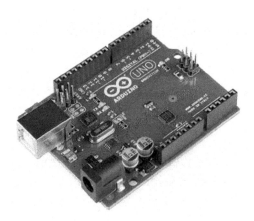

LM35 Temperature Sensor

LM35 is a 3 stick temperature sensor which gives 1 degree Celsius on each 10mVolt change. This sensor can detect up to 150 degree Celsius temperature. 1 number stick of lm35 sensor is Vcc, second is yield and third one is Ground.

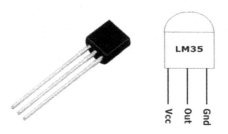

Pin No	Function	Name
1	Supply voltage; 5V (+35V to -2V)	Vcc
2	Output voltage (+6V to -1V)	Output
3	Ground (0V)	Ground

LCD

16x2 LCD unit is generally utilizing in inserted framework ventures since it is modest, effectively availablet, little in size and simple to interface. 16x2 have two lines and 16 sections, which implies it comprise 16 squares of 5x8 specks. 16 stick for associations in which 8 information bits D0-D7 and 3 control bits to be specific RS, RW and EN. Rest of pins are utilized for supply, splendor control and for backdrop illumination.

Power Supply

Arduino Board as of now have an inbuilt power supply segment. Here we just need to interface a 9 volt or 12 volt connectors with the board.

Circuit Diagram and Explanation

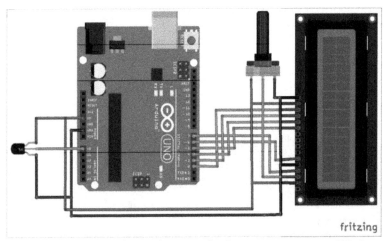

Circuit digram for advanced thermometer utilizing Arduino LM35 temperature sensor, is appeared in the above figure. Make the associations cautiously as appeared in the schematic. Here 16x2 LCD unit is legitimately associated with arduino in 4-piece mode. Information pins of LCD to be specific RS, EN, D4, D5, D6, D7 are associated with arduino advanced stick number 7, 6, 5, 4, 3, 2. A temperature sensor LM35 is additionally associated with Analog stick A0 of arduino, which creates 1 degree Celsius temperature on each 10mV yield change at its yield stick.

Arduino LM35 Code & Explanation

To compose the code for computerized thermometer, we have to compose the code for Arduino, LM35 Temperature Sensor, as well as 16x2 LCD module interfacing. First we incorporate library for LCD unit and afterward we characterizes information and control pins for LCD and temperature sensor.

```
#include<LiquidCrystal.h>
LiquidCrystal lcd(7,6,5,4,3,2);

#define sensor A0
```

Subsequent to getting simple esteem at simple stick we peruses that worth utilizing Analog read capacity and stores that incentive in a variable. And afterward by applying given recipe changes over it in temperature.

skim analog_value=analogRead(analog_pin);

skim Temperature=analog_value*factor*100

where

factor=5/1023

analog_value = yield of temperature sensor

```
/*---------Temperature-------*/
    float reading=analogRead(sensor);
    float temperature=reading*(5.0/1023.0)*100;
    delay(10);
```

Here degree image is makes utilizing custom character technique

```
byte degree[8] =
            {
                0b00011,
                0b00011,
                0b00000,
                0b00000,
                0b00000,
                0b00000,
                0b00000,
                0b00000
            };
```

Code

```
/*-----------Arduino LM35 Code-------------*/
/*-----------Digital      Thermometer      Using      Ar-
duino------------*/
#include<LiquidCrystal.h>
LiquidCrystal lcd(7,6,5,4,3,2);
#define sensor A0
byte degree[8] =
    {
    0b00011,
    0b00011,
    0b00000,
    0b00000,
    0b00000,
```

```
        0b00000,
        0b00000,
        0b00000
      };
void setup()
{
 lcd.begin(16,2);
 lcd.createChar(1, degree);
 lcd.setCursor(0,0);
 lcd.print(" Digital  ");
 lcd.setCursor(0,1);
 lcd.print(" Thermometer ");
 delay(4000);
 lcd.clear();
 lcd.print(" Hello World");
 delay(4000);
 lcd.clear();
}
void loop()
{
 /*---------Temperature-------*/
   float reading=analogRead(sensor);
   float temperature=reading*(5.0/1023.0)*100;
   delay(10);


   /*------Display Result------*/
   lcd.clear();
   lcd.setCursor(2,0);
   lcd.print("Temperature");
   lcd.setCursor(4,1);
```

```
lcd.print(temperature);
lcd.write(1);
lcd.print("C");
delay(1000);
}
```

www.ingramcontent.com/pod-product-compliance
Lightning Source LLC
Chambersburg PA
CBHW070846070326
40690CB00009B/1717